Finding the Calm

Finding the Calm

Biblical Meditations to Nourish Those Who Nurture Teens

David Haas

Saint Mary's Press
Winona, Minnesota

Genuine recycled paper with 10% post-consumer waste.
Printed with soy-based ink. 50636

The publishing team included Laurie Delgatto, development editor; Brooke
E. Saron, copy editor and production editor; Barbara Bartelson, typesetter;
Andy Palmer and Cären Yang, art directors and designers; Jonathan Thomas
Goebel, cover designer; cover image, SuperStock; inside image, copyright
Artville, LLC; manufacturing coordinated by the production services depart-
ment of Saint Mary's Press.

The acknowledgments continue on page 92.

Printed in the United States of America

Printing: 9 8 7 6 5 4 3 2 1

Year: 2011 10 09 08 07 06 05 04 03

ISBN 0-88489-792-3

Library of Congress Cataloging-in-Publication Data

Haas, David.
    Finding the calm : biblical meditations to nourish those who nurture
teens / David Haas.
        p. cm.
Includes index.
ISBN 0-88489-792-3 (pbk.)
    1. Church work with teenagers. 2. Teenagers—Religious life. I.
Title.
BV4447 .H28 2003
242'.69—dc21
                                                                2002014394

Contents

Author acknowledgments

There are many who deserve thanks for helping to bring this book to life. I especially want to thank my dear friend, Scripture professor, fellow writer, and collaborator, Arthur Zannoni. Art has been most influential in my appreciation as to how the Scriptures are a foundational font and source for all ministerial formation, regardless of the particular discipline. I also want to thank my friend and mentor Sr. Gertrude Foley, SC, who years ago helped me to understand the need for critical thinking and reflection as an important partner alongside ministerial zeal and passion. I am deeply grateful to both of them for their inspiration, witness, friendship, and encouragement.

I also want to thank Tony Alonso; Leisa Anslinger; Fr. Jim Bessert; Anita Bradshaw; Joe Camacho; Barbara Conley-Waldmiller; Kate Cuddy; Fr. George DeCosta; Fr. Ray East; Tom Franzak; Rob and Mary Glover; Bill Huebsch; Jo Infante; Sr. Roberta Kolasa, SJ; Sr. Andrea Lee, IHM; Stephen Petrunak; Carol Porter; Sr. Kathleen Storms, SSND; Rob Strusinski; Mary Werner; Jackie Witter; and all who regularly support my ministerial work through their friendship, loyalty, challenge, and love. I also wish to express my gratitude to friends and colleagues who truly inspire me in their love and work with youth: Eileen Bird, Jeffrey and Jean Bross-Judge, Ian Callanan, Derek Campbell, Sue Cipolle, Tom East, Bobby Fisher, Connie Fourre, Jim Hamburge, Alissa Hetzner, Mike Jeremiah, Paul Keefe, Marilee Mahler, Jesse Manibusan, Tricia Nolan, Colleen Riley, Anna Scally, Paul Tate, and Bob Tift. Important thanks and gratitude go to Lori True, for her love, friendship, and support, for her always being an endless river of ideas and help in so many of my ministerial projects, and for her tremendous love and passion for young people. I am also grateful to the faith community of Saint Cecilia's Parish in Saint Paul, Minnesota, and to the faculty and students of Benilde-Saint Margaret's School in Saint Louis Park, Minnesota.

Many, many thanks to the people of Saint Mary's Press, especially Laurie Delgatto, good friend and editor of this project, as well as

Brian Singer-Towns and Steve Nagel for their encouragement and helpful suggestions. Their commitment to developing quality resources for the youth ministry community is unparalleled. I am proud to be a part of their mission. And, of course, love and thanks go to my parents, who truly were the best youth ministers I ever had, and to Helen, for her love and helpful suggestions in the writing of this manuscript.

Finally, I would like to thank so many young people from whom I have learned much in recent years, especially Teresa Arisco; Chuck Bennincasa; Ben and Emily Byers-Ferrian; Bridgette Catino; Anne Chesny; Frances Churchill; Marty Coffman; Melissa Cuddy; Clare Diegel; Janene Dold; Dave Doppell; Colleen Dukinfield; John Eichten; Mike Fabiano; Katie Fleischhacker; Ria Flom; Bridgette Frantz; Nathan Hetrick; Sarah Hudetz; Steve Kron; Patti Lotz; Jake, Laura, and Mike Mahler; Katie McGinty; Kevin O'Connor; Jonathan Phang; Matt Reichert; Bobby Reuter; Joel Samuels; Lori Snook; Jordan Snyder; Zack Stachowski; Erin Wencl; Grace Wenk; Tim Westerhaus; and Paul Ziezulewicz. They and so many other young people have taught me so much. Their lives and yearning for growth, more than any other resource, have influenced the meditations found in these pages. It is to them, and to the fulfillment of their dreams that this book is dedicated.

Introduction

Those of us engaged in ministry to and with youth are constantly looking for more effective ways to reach out and help them discover the caring hand of God in their life. Because we ourselves have come to know the power of God's presence, we desperately want young people to know and experience what we know, both now at this unique time of their journey and in the future that lies ahead for each of them.

Adolescents are aching for an awesome and radical God to fall in love with. Because too many young people rarely discover this God, they seek out other answers, other paths. They look to us to reveal to them something special, something beyond what they already see, know, touch, and experience. We try so many things—programs, pizza parties, "relevant" liturgies and retreats—but most seem to fall short. With good intentions we often reach out in a reactive mode, attending to short-term needs and situations rather than offering our youth a true spiritual path for their lives.

Ministry is not something we "do" but rather it is a radical way of living in relationship to God and in response to one another. Far too often we trade in holiness for "what works," for what is successful. This might work in short-term circumstances, but in the long haul, many of our young people are still lost. And much of the time, we ministers lose our way as well.

We need to rediscover and commit ourselves to the fundamental energy of ministry: prayer. For many people, prayer is often an excuse or an escape in ministry. The thought often seems to be that action, "doing something," is where our priorities should be. However, without having a true discipline and posture of prayer at the center of all our activity, burnout far too often becomes a painful result. In working with youth, this is even more evident because of pastors', parents', and others' expectations for results. Determining our ministerial goals and measuring our success in terms of prayer and spiritual life is difficult. Yet we have to correct the notion that being a person of prayer is a passive activity, an activity that removes a person from the reality of life. To be a prayerful person, especially in the biblical sense, is to be a person who is integrated, focused, and connected, and whose actions come from a place of vision.

What young people need and are yearning to see from adults is a way of life steeped in a different way of living, an alternative way that influences their choices, a unique lifestyle that makes sense amidst the madness of this world. Now, more than ever, our young people desperately need the witness of adults who truly believe, not only with their words but also through the intentionality of their behavior, in the power of prayer and reflection in their lives. Our young people need adult leaders who are prophetic, committed "spokespeople for God." Our young people deserve to hear this kind of prophetic voice. They need to see that the power of the Word is more than arbitrary Bible verses being thrown at them like quotes from a magazine. They need and deserve the richness of the Scriptures as a true icon for living life in Christ Jesus.

The marriage of the Scriptures and prayer is the focus of these reflections. Each reflection begins with a passage from the Scriptures followed by a short meditation, a prayer, and some questions for reflection. The reflections can be used individually or in a group setting with other ministers and leaders. Be creative in your approach to using them. Try to use them in a regular daily pattern if you can, and read them aloud if possible.

My own personal prayer style is conversational, so the prayers that follow the meditations reflect my own personal journey of growth and experience that I both celebrate and struggle with. I hope that these meditations and prayers can help embolden and empower you in the crazy and complicated world of reaching out to young people. May we all remember that God is in charge and that one of the most important energies in ministry is to listen well and respond honestly with passion and commitment.

This book is for all of you who minister to and with young people, including professional youth ministers, volunteers, parents, pastors, teachers, and catechists and mentors. I hope this book can be a resource for those of you who strive to have your ministerial work and your prayer life more integrated. May these reflections help nurture, sustain, and challenge your commitment to youth. Let us pray—always.

Pass on the call
to ministry

Scripture Passage

Moses did as the LORD had commanded him. Taking Joshua and having him stand in the presence of the priest Eleazar and of the whole community, he laid his hands on him and gave him his commission, as the LORD had directed through Moses.

(Numbers 27:22–23)

Meditation

One of the most important aspects of ministry is the challenge and charge that we have to call others to share in the task—to empower and form others to work in the vineyard. One of the things we may forget to do is to recognize the spark to serve that many of our young people have as well. We are called to affirm and apprentice these young spirits to the same call that we have been given. We need to "lay hands" and bless the potential that we see—that the Lord sees—and set it free.

Prayer

God,
help me not become stuck
or too enamored
with my own gifts,
my own call,
and my own status.
I need you to continually
provoke within me the mandate
to see as you see
the gifts and talents of our young people,
and to challenge them
to respond and serve your people.
Help me to respond to the light
that you have given them—
and watch them lead.
Amen.

Questions for Reflection

ℓ How do I unintentionally keep young people from utilizing their own gifts?

ℓ What more can I do to empower youth to take their place as ministers?

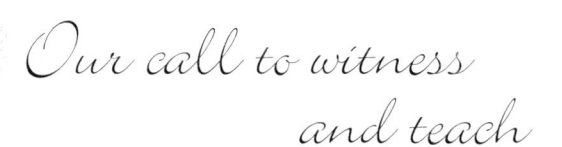

Our call to witness and teach

Scripture Passage

Take care and be earnestly on your guard not to forget the things which your own eyes have seen, nor let them slip from your memory as long as you live, but teach them to your children and to your children's children.

(Deuteronomy 4:9)

Meditation

Good stories need to be shared. We need to impart to young people the tremendous stories of our faith. We are called to witness with passion and enthusiasm the events and experiences that have helped to shape who we are, what we believe, and what we hope to accomplish in our lives. We have received the gift of our experiences, both the blessings and the flaws, and they are not for us to keep to ourselves for our own selfish needs or patterns of growth. Often they occur so that someone else can learn and grow as well. When we share these treasures with our young people, they will be the better for it. This is what it means to be a teacher: to live fully and witness fully.

Prayer

God,
help me to be attentive, to remember,
and hold close to my heart
the stirrings, experiences, and events
that have been planted in my life.
Help me to pass them on to the young people
whom you have entrusted to my care.
Help me to be willing to reveal
some of the chapters of my life.
Hopefully, in the sharing
we all will see you in a new way.
Amen.

Questions for Reflection

℮ What is my story of faith? What are the experiences that have shaped who I am?

℮ How do I share this story with the young people in my life?

God's story is their story

Scripture Passage

Friends,
let me begin with a story,
an old story
that has been shared
and passed down
from generation to generation.
We must always remember
to share this story with everyone we can.
God has taken care of us always,
and that message must continue.
Let your friends and children learn
that God can be trusted,
that God's way is the only way.

(Psalm-prayer 78, Haas,
Prayers Before an Awesome God, page 73)

Meditation

Far too often, young people feel that God's promise is only for a people who lived long ago—that the people whom God reached out to
in the Bible somehow were unique in receiving God's fidelity and
love. The story of God's promise, God's Covenant, and God's everlasting, unconditional love is an unending story, not limited to a particular time or space, and certainly not limited to a certain group of
people. It is a promise and a story for all of us. Young people need to
somehow feel that they are truly worthy of hearing and receiving
God's salvation and redemption. God wants to reach them, and we
are called to be a mouthpiece for that message.

Prayer

God,
help me be the living Word,
a vital, passionate witness
of the wonderful story of your love,
your mercy,
your redemption,
and your promise.
Speak within me.
Help my voice and life be clear.
Give me the strength and the joy
to open the eyes, the hearts,
and the minds of our young people.
We can do this together,
for you are with me.
Show me the way.
Give me the words.
Help me share the story.
Amen.

Questions for Reflection

- ℯ How can I embrace the Word more deeply in my life and ministry?
- ℯ What are the ways in which I can impart the richness of the Scriptures with young people?

God's awesome way with us

Scripture Passage

Bless the LORD, O my soul,
    and all that is within me,
    bless his holy name.
Bless the LORD, O my soul,
    and do not forget all his benefits—
who forgives all your iniquity,
    who heals all your diseases,
who redeems your life from the Pit,
    who crowns you with steadfast love and mercy,
who satisfies you with good as long as you live
    so that your youth is renewed like the eagle's.

. . . .

The LORD is merciful and gracious,
    slow to anger and abounding in steadfast love.
He will not always accuse,
    nor will he keep his anger forever.
He does not deal with us according to our sins,
    nor repay us according to our iniquities.
For as the heavens are high above the earth,
    so great is his steadfast love toward those who fear him;
as far as the east is from the west,
    so far he removes our transgressions from us.
As a father has compassion for his children,
    so the LORD has compassion for those who fear him.

(Psalm 103:1–5,8–13)

Meditation

It is hard to imagine or comprehend that our God is as generous as this Scripture passage proclaims, but it is true. Our God is amazing and incomprehensible in putting up with us, in forgiving us over and over again, and in constantly seeing the best and the possible in each of us. This God does so much more than we can imagine. God forgives, heals, and redeems. God crowns us and satisfies us. This awesome and incredible God is slow to anger and will not deal with us in the way that we deserve but rather will remove our transgressions and lavishly cover us with compassion. Sad as it may be, our young people are too often filled with self-loathing, poor self-esteem, and hopelessness when they look at themselves. They desperately need to hear this good news. They need to know about this God, whose relationship with them is unlike any other relationship they could ever possibly have. Those of us in ministry have hopefully had many glimpses of this loving God. Let's make sure our young people hear the story as well.

Prayer

God,
time and time again,
you constantly overwhelm me
with your unconditional
forgiveness and faithfulness.
You never give up on me.
You are always close, always loving.
You are always healing and lifting me up
beyond anything I deserve,
beyond anything I could hope for,
beyond anything that I could imagine from you.
Help me to be that same presence,
to be the same way with the young people in my life.

Help me to always see the best in them,
to shower them with my own belief in them
and in all that they can be.
Help me to help them
see and experience you as I have.
Faithful.
Always.
Amen.

Questions for Reflection

℃ Do I really believe that God loves me unconditionally?

℃ Which young people in my community, parish, or school need most to receive and experience this kind of love?

The desire for insight

Scripture Passage

My child, if you accept my words
    and treasure up my commandments within you,
making your ear attentive to wisdom
    and inclining your heart to understanding;
if you indeed cry out for insight,
    and raise your voices for understanding;
if you seek it like silver,
    and search for it as for hidden treasures—
then you will understand the fear of the LORD
    and find the knowledge of God.
For the LORD gives wisdom;
    from his mouth come knowledge and understanding;
he stores up sound wisdom for the upright;
    he is a shield to those who walk blamelessly,
guarding the paths of justice
    and preserving the way of his faithful ones.
Then you will understand righteousness and justice
    and equity, every good path;
for wisdom will come into your heart,
    and knowledge will be pleasant to your soul;
prudence will watch over you;
    and understanding will guard you.
It will save you from the way of evil,
    from those who speak perversely. . . .

. . . .

Therefore walk in the way of the good,
    and keep to the paths of the just.

(Proverbs 2:1–12,20)

Meditation

One of the greatest aches that young people long for—whether we see it or not—is insight and wisdom. They long to find adults and mentors who they can emulate. Sometimes they look for heroes, and oftentimes their expectations are too high. But most of the time, they are looking just for integrity—they want to experience and develop relationships with adults who, at minimum, try. They seek to find something to believe in, adults who do try, with a sense of balance and altruism. They do not need us to have all the answers; they do not ask us to be perfect. They just want to know that, like them, we are trying, and that it is worth the effort.

Prayer

God,
help me, above all things,
to live my life with integrity.
Give me an eager heart
that yearns and longs for wisdom—
your wisdom.
Give me a generous heart
that lavishly reaches out to do what is right.
Give me a patient heart
that forgives me when I falter
and calms me when I am impatient.
If my heart is open to your wisdom,
I can truly know insight
and come closer to you.
Then those who look up to me
will not be disappointed.
Show me your way.
Amen.

Questions for Reflection

- When young people see the way I live, what do I think they really see?
- Who were the mentors and heroes that I had when I was young?
- What was it about them that inspired me?

The path of calm

Scripture Passage

My child, do not let these escape from your sight:
    keep sound wisdom and prudence,
and they will be life for your soul
    and adornment for your neck.
Then you will walk on your way securely
    and your foot will not stumble.
If you sit down, you will not be afraid;
    when you lie down, your sleep will be sweet.
Do not be afraid of sudden panic,
    or of the storm that strikes the wicked;
for the LORD will be your confidence
    and will keep your foot from being caught.

(Proverbs 3:21–26)

Meditation

Living the spiritual life is sometimes less about what we think of God and more about whether we can sleep at night. God wants to free us from our anxiety, so God calls upon us to remember that the times of peril we experience are finite and that we are not alone through it all. God will be there—if we allow God in. We need to keep breathing, to be fully human, and to ask God to be with us in our fear. Young people live in terrifying times. They worry too much, and with each generation comes more pressure, more anxiety, more stress, and, in many cases, more violence and premature death. We need to show young people an alternative to this crazy path of nonsense— first by practicing it ourselves.

Prayer

God,
I need calm.
Our young people need calm,
the calm and confidence that you alone can give.
Help us to receive it.
Help us to remember
that you are with us.
Help us to lean on you
and to remember that when stress comes
you will be there to help us rise above the struggle.
We will endure because you are always present.
Help us to remember that.
Amen.

Questions for Reflection

- What are the things that paralyze me in my calling?
- How can I be more attentive to the worries and anxieties of young people?

 *Keep the vision*

Scripture Passage

Where there is no vision the people get out of hand.

(Proverbs 29:18)

Meditation

In the hustle and franticness of our daily activities and tasks, it is seductive to lose the vision and to forget to keep our "eyes on the prize." We need to provide young people with a vision. A vision for how they can live their lives with meaning; a vision for how they can age well and make good choices; a vision for how they can survive. What is that vision? It is Jesus the Christ—not just the man who lived, taught, and performed miracles in his day, but the Christ who lives beyond history, the Christ who is more than a historical person, the Christ who is more significantly the Risen Lord. This Lord who transcends human history proclaims a way of life that contradicts the wisdom of the world, the culture, and the frailties of human nature. Let's not lose the vision—let us hold fast to Jesus, who is our brother, who is the Christ.

Prayer

God,
you are the center of my life,
you are the center of all things.
Far too often I get sidetracked,
and I become too preoccupied with work,
with success, with numbers,
with reaching the finish line of my parish program,
and with pleasing the pastor and parents.
Help me to remain focused on the vision—your vision.
For you come to me to show me how to live,
not for me to be buried in my work and duties.
Keep the way clear.
Help me to remember your vision.
Amen.

Questions for Reflection

- *C* What are the ways in which my work can get in the way of my spiritual life and growth?
- *C* What rhythms, disciplines, or patterns can I nurture within myself in order to keep the balance even?

The call to advocacy

Scripture Passage

Speak out for those who cannot speak.

(Proverbs 31:8)

Meditation

While young people certainly are filled with their opinions, they hardly have a voice that can penetrate the voices of those who often want to destroy their dreams—the voices of those who feel the need to bring them down to size, the voices of those who refuse to listen to their hopes and desires. In the world and even in the Church, young people are often kept at the boundaries and told "You are not ready yet," or "It is not your time," or "You do not know what is good for you." Young people are imbued with a wonderful sense of passion, and they have gifts and wisdom that we (not always intentionally) refuse or are unable to see, hear, or recognize. One of our most important roles is being an advocate. We need to speak out on behalf of young people to those who "don't get it," who want to keep them at the periphery of life. Young people want to act; they want to get their hands dirty, they are longing to get into the mix. They need our help.

Prayer

God,
our young people are reaching out.
They are often ready and willing,
sometimes confident, sometimes scared,
sometimes lacking direction.
But they have energy—energy to be tapped,
an energy that can so easily be snuffed out.
Help me,
help all of us who have a voice,
be a herald and proclamation
for those young people in our midst
who need our help to blaze a trail for them.
Help me use my voice
so they can be heard.
Amen.

Questions for Reflection

℮ Who are the young ones in my community who have no voice?

℮ How can I be a stronger and more effective advocate for them?

God's plan for their future

Scripture Passage

For surely I know the plans I have for you, says the LORD, plans for your welfare not for woe! plans to give you a future full of hope. When you call me, when you go to pray to me, I will listen to you. When you look for me, you will find me. Yes, when you seek me with all your heart, you will find me with you, says the LORD.

(Jeremiah 29:11–14)

Meditation

Our young people need hope. The prime time in which that hope can be made known to them is, paradoxically, when things seem hopeless. When everything seems to be going wrong, when everything seems to be closing in, when everything seems to be filled with hurt, pain, and suffering—that is when hope needs to be infused in young people's lives. That is when young people are most receptive to hear God's voice and most able to receive a word of hope—a word of hope different from the hope that other forces in the world attempt to give. Thinking that we adults are the hope would be arrogant, inappropriate, and harmful on our part. We are not this hope. At best we are the messengers of this hope. We have to remind our young people (and ourselves) that they have a future, and it might be one that is in opposition to their original plans, but there is a plan. God's plan. Not ours. And God's plan is better than ours.

Prayer

God,
please be with our young people
in their searching, in their confusion,
in their worry and anxiety.
Help them to see
beyond the terror that they may be going through
and to see you with them,
holding on to them through it all.
May I be an instrument of the hope that you are.
Amen.

Questions for Reflection

- Where and in whom do I place my hope?
- Am I an authentic messenger of hope to the young people in my community?

# God's Covenant

Scripture Passage

You shall be my people,
and I will be your God.

(Jeremiah 30:22)

Meditation

We are the people of God. We need to notice from this Scripture passage that God does not give an age requirement for this status. In other words, our young people need to feel and experience themselves as being integral parts of this family of God, and often, unfortunately, they do not. They are not on training wheels, they are first-class citizens in the community of faith. How are we, however unconsciously, keeping them at bay? Are we doing all that we can to bring them into the mainstream of all aspects of family, parish, and faith life? Young people are God's people. We need to treat them as such and provide opportunities and open doors for them to enter and take their place.

Prayer

God,
you show no partiality,
for we are all your people,
and we all belong to you.
Help us all to welcome all
to feel your presence.
Help our young people feel
that they belong to us,
to you, and to the Church.
Help us all to be one in you,
your people,
your missionaries,
and your presence to the world.
May all of us,
young and old,
remember our identity:
God's People.
What an awesome gift.
Help us to never forget.
Amen.

Questions for Reflection

- *C* What are the policies and practices in my community that might be holding youth back?
- *C* Which young people in my community need extra encouragement and affirmation?

The prophecy of young people

Scripture Passage

After this
I shall pour out my spirit on all humanity.
Your sons and daughters shall prophesy,
your old people shall dream dreams,
and your young people see visions.

(Joel 3:1)

Meditation

Our young people have so much to offer to us and the Church. If we would only take more time to listen, with open ears and hearts, we could learn so much from them. Our Church is always in need of renewal, and our young people can help show the way, but we need to make sure the microphone is on when they come forward to speak. Let's listen more to their ideas and creativity, and let's allow their enthusiasm and optimism to lead the way. They have a message, and they probably have many of the solutions that we as a broken, sinful, and needy Church need to hear.

Prayer

God,
open our ears,
open our hearts,
open our hands
to embrace the gifts of our young people.
We know and believe
that you bless them
and live within their hopes, dreams, and ideals.
Help us to embrace their wisdom,
open our memories to recall
that we were young once ourselves,
and that we too
were desperate to be heard,
and to have someone listen to us.
Break through,
and help our young people break through as well
so that we may see the world and Church
as they see it—
and learn.
Amen.

Questions for Reflection

℃ Who are the true young prophets in our midst?
℃ What can I do to be an advocate for them?

 *Worship with integrity*

Scripture Passage

I hate, I despise your festivals,
  and I take no delight in your solemn assemblies.
Even though you offer me your burnt offerings and grain offerings,
  I will not accept them;
and the offerings of well-being of your fatted animals
  I will not look upon.
Take away from me the noise of your songs;
  I will not listen to the melody of your harps.
But let justice roll down like waters,
  and righteousness like an ever-flowing stream.

(Amos 5:21–24)

Meditation

Young people have the abilities to discern and to think critically. They can see through hypocrisy, phoniness, and inconsistency. They see how our prayers, hymns, and "sacred actions" do not always measure up to the way we live our lives. Sunday morning seems like a drop in the bucket alongside the rest of the week when we do not live up to what we proclaim in our prayer. While we have to remind young people that we as believers are never perfect in living up to the words we pray and the songs we sing, we too have to realize the immense responsibility that we have. Our prayer, our liturgy, will not speak to young people unless they see that we will live by the creeds and beliefs we utter. Upbeat music or hip services will not attract our youth to the worship life of the Church, but the integrity with which we live up to our rituals will.

Prayer

God,

we pray and we sing,

but our prayer is empty to your ears

unless we take up the challenge to live

as people of justice, as people of mercy,

as people who bring about change

and reconciliation in our families, our communities,

and to the stranger and the outcast.

Help us.

Give us the strength to proclaim your kingdom

where the poor are fed, where the lonely are no longer abandoned,

where the abused are healed, and where all can live in peace.

Then we will truly have something to sing about,

and then you will truly be praised, as you should be.

Be with us in the struggle, and then your children will follow.

Amen.

Questions for Reflection

℮ Are we selling our youth short, or do our liturgies proclaim the truth?

℮ What am I doing to bridge the gap between liturgy and social justice in all aspects of parish life?

 *Welcome our youth*

Scripture Passage

Taking a child he placed it in their midst, and putting his arms around it he said to them, "Whoever receives one child such as this in my name, receives me; and whoever receives me, receives not me but the One who sent me."

(Mark 9:36–37)

Meditation

A young person approached a youth minister and asked: "If I did not come to Sunday Mass for about a month, would I be missed?" This is a common concern of young people. They desperately need to know that they matter, that they are important, that they are worthwhile. We need to embrace, welcome, and lavish our young people with a sense of how wonderful and important they really are. To be a welcoming people means that we have to go out of our way for someone else, and our youth need this more than anyone. They (and all of us) need to have a sense that if they are not with us, we are less than the whole Body of Christ.

Prayer

God,
help me to reach outside of myself,
to be extra conscious of the young who ache
to feel connected to you
and to your people.
Help me to welcome as you welcome,
not just with "hello"
but rather
with a true and authentic sense of welcome
that honors, reveres,
and recognizes that you are with us,
in all things, in all people.
Help me to see you in them.
Amen.

Questions for Reflection

- How do the youth in my community feel about their membership and identity within the parish?
- What can I do to help integrate the youth as full, first-class citizens in my community?

Let the children come to me

Scripture Passage

"Let the children come to me; do not prevent them, for the kingdom of God belongs to such as these. Amen, I say to you, whoever does not accept the kingdom of God like a child will not enter it." Then he embraced them and blessed them, placing his hands on them.

(Mark 10:14–16)

Meditation

As we grow older, it is easy to lose our optimism, to lose our vision, to become cynical and forget the dream. We need to walk alongside our young people, learn from them, and challenge them to lead the way. We need them. We need their youthfulness, their energy, their outrageousness, and their joy. They are often confused by some of the things that seem to preoccupy our priorities. They do not always understand the battles and conflicts that we choose to become embroiled in. Let us all embrace some of their ideas, their thoughts, and their creativity. And ask them to embrace us and pray for us as well.

Prayer

God,
help me,
help us all to see the world
through the eyes of a child.
Help us to let go of our perceived wisdom,
our addiction to be right,
and our need to feel that our young people
have to listen to our wisdom only.
Bring a conversion to us now,
and help us to remember
that we have so much to learn from young people.
Help us listen to them.
In doing so we will learn more about you.
Amen.

Questions for Reflection

- What and who are the influences in my life that keep me from remaining positive?
- Which young people in my community have something to teach me?

Mary: model for youth

Scripture Passage

And Mary said:

"My soul proclaims the greatness of the Lord;
    my spirit rejoices in God my savior.
For he has looked upon his
      handmaid's lowliness;
    behold, from now on will all ages call me blessed.
The Mighty One has done great things for me,
    and holy is his name.
His mercy is from age to age
    to those who fear him.
He has shown might with his arm,
    dispersed the arrogant of mind and heart.
He has thrown down the rulers from their thrones,
    but lifted up the lowly.
The hungry he has filled with good things;
    the rich he has sent away empty.
He has helped Israel his servant,
    remembering his mercy,
according to his promise to our fathers,
    to Abraham and to his
      descendants forever."

(Luke 1:46–55)

Meditation

It is a wonderful metaphor for youth ministry to see a teenage girl as the primary agent for God breaking into the world. Mary proclaims the presence of God by more than just biologically bringing Jesus into the world. She does so by announcing and challenging all to embrace the same mission to which she herself is called. This is the essence of ministry—to witness to the community our common mission, first by proclamation, then by example. Like the Greek metaphor for Mary, *Theotokos* (which means the "God-bearer"), we are called to do more than talk about Jesus—we are called to "bear" that presence to our young people.

Prayer

God,
you continually do great things for us,
and as you are holy, you call us to be a beacon of holiness to the world.
Come now, and help me to truly magnify your name
through proclaiming to young people your mercy and justice
by the entirety of my life.
Call me, prod me, and seduce me every day
to truly be your disciple.
Amen.

Questions for Reflection

℃ How am I a living "yes" and witness to and for young people?
℃ What ways can I be more effective as a "God-bearer" in my life?

God's destiny
for all young people

Scripture Passage

"Blessed be the Lord, the God of Israel,
   for he has visited and brought redemption to his people.
He has raised up a horn for our salvation
   within the house of David his servant,
      even as he promised through the mouth of his holy
         prophets from of old:
      salvation from our enemies and from the hand
         of all who hate us,
to show mercy to our fathers
   and to be mindful of his holy covenant
and of the oath he swore to Abraham our father,
   and to grant us that,
      rescued from the hand of enemies,
without fear we might worship him
   in holiness and righteousness
   before him all our days.
And you, child, will be called prophet of the Most High,
   for you will go before the Lord to prepare his ways,
to give his people knowledge of salvation
   through the forgiveness of their sins,
because of the tender mercy of our God
   by which the daybreak from on high will visit us
to shine on those who sit in darkness and death's shadow,
   to guide our feet into the path of peace."

(Luke 1:68–79)

Meditation

In this wonderful canticle, Zechariah proclaims the mission of John
the Baptist, the mission that all of us are compelled to emulate. Those

who minister to youth are like John the Baptist—the one who points beyond himself to the one who truly is the Savior, Jesus Christ. Like John, we are called to prepare the way of the Lord, clearly acknowledging that Jesus is Lord and we are not. However, it is not the relief that we feel that as a John the Baptist we find out we are not the savior—it is much more than that. It is our responsibility to do as John did—to point others, especially our young people during this vulnerable time of their life, to Jesus Christ.

Prayer

God,
you call me to prepare the way,
to point beyond myself, to Jesus,
your way, your marvelous truth, and your light of life.
Help me to live your light in the midst of the sorrow and anxiety
that often surrounds the lives of our young people.
Help me to keep pointing to your Son,
and then they (and I) will be led forth
into the way of your peace.
Amen.

Questions for Reflection

- In all my work and ministry, do I become the point, or do I point beyond?
- Which young people in my community are or have the potential to be messengers?

# The call of God's spirit

Scripture Passage

He unrolled the scroll and found the passage where it was written:
    "The Spirit of the Lord is upon me,
        because he has anointed me
            to bring glad tidings to the poor.
    He has sent me to proclaim liberty to captives
        and recovery of sight to the blind,
            to let the oppressed go free,
        and to proclaim a year acceptable to the Lord."
Rolling up the scroll, he handed it back to the attendant and sat down, and the eyes of all in the synagogue looked intently at him. He said to them, "Today this scripture passage is fulfilled in your hearing."
(Luke 4:17–21)

Meditation

We need to hear good news, and our young people need to hear good news in the midst of a world that presents them with so much bad news. Their discouragement, their worry about the future, their anxiety about their lives, relationships, and sense of self all ache for a glimmer of light that seems absent so much of the time. Young people need to know that this promise is more than some distant possibility if and when they get to heaven. They need to know that this hope is possible now. Let us all keep giving them this hope—not a naive, giddy sort of utopia but rather a promise that something better lies on the other side, no matter what pain and struggles possess them at this moment.

Prayer

God,
you call me,
and you call all of us,
to share in the mission of your Son.
You created each and every one of us
to become your Good News.
You breathed life into our souls
so that we may carry out the mission
that your Word-made-flesh, Jesus the Christ,
planted into the spirit of the world.
Help us to proclaim your year of favor,
to all of us, young and old.
May we fulfill your Word.
Amen.

Questions for Reflection

⊘ What are the events and situations taking place in the world and in everyday life that keep young people from being hopeful and positive?

⊘ Where do I see good news among youth? Am I bringing it to light?

The mission

Scripture Passage

He summoned the Twelve and gave them power and authority over all demons and to cure diseases, and he sent them to proclaim the kingdom of God and to heal [the sick]. He said to them, "Take nothing for the journey, neither walking stick, nor sack, nor food, nor money, and let no one take a second tunic. Whatever house you enter, stay there and leave from there. And as for those who do not welcome you, when you leave that town, shake the dust from your feet in testimony against them." Then they set out and went from village to village proclaiming the good news and curing diseases everywhere.

(Luke 9:1–6)

Meditation

Certain people come into ministry with a romantic sense of purpose. They have visions of grandeur, of lofty actions and results. Yes, the rewards of ministry and service are many, but the cost and lifestyle bring peril and hardship at times, and it is often anything but romantic or glamorous. We are called to detach from things that are not important—material things such as clothing or money or anything that gives us a false sense of comfort. Working with young people requires detachment from things that can get in the way of our truly being present to them during this critical time in their lives. We need to stay focused and not let the trappings of comfort and convenience take precedence.

Prayer

God,
help me to let go.
Help me to let go of the things
that I think I really need.
While resources, workshops, programs,
curriculums, and consultants are helpful,
they are not the most important things.
What young people need the most is my love;
my attention; and my reverencing who they are,
what they long for, and their search for you.
May I always strip away the things
that get in the way.
May I always bring
the Good News—your Good News.
Amen.

Questions for Reflection

℮ How do I sometimes hide in the trappings of life?
℮ How can I break through the things that get in the way of my
   deeper calling?

God is running toward our youth

Scripture Passage

While he was still a long way off, his father caught sight of him, and was filled with compassion. He ran to his son, embraced him and kissed him. His son said to him, "Father, I have sinned against heaven and against you; I no longer deserve to be called your son." But his father ordered his servants, "Quickly bring the finest robe and put it on him; put a ring on his finger and sandals on his feet. Take the fattened calf and slaughter it. Then let us celebrate with a feast, because this son of mine was dead, and has come to life again; he was lost, and has been found." Then the celebration began.

(Luke 15:20–24)

Meditation

Our God does more than forgive our young people when they falter; God does more than just wait for them to return and make good choices. God is always running toward them, embracing them, and adorning them with the finest love. The amazing thing about our God is that when we fail we experience this love even more lavishly. One of the most difficult things for young people to deal with is knowing or feeling that they have disappointed us. Will we respond with indignation or with forgiveness and celebration that they have grown and have picked themselves up again? The call of Jesus is to celebrate and robe them with joy and love. We need to do the same.

Prayer

God,
you never repay us in the way we deserve.
You are always moving toward us,
and you do not haunt us with our mistakes.
Rather, you celebrate our growth.
May I be that same presence,
may I do the same
for myself, for others,
and for those who come to me,
asking for a blessing in their worst of times.
Help me to always celebrate young people,
not judge them.
Amen.

Questions for Reflection

- When in my life have I experienced God truly embracing me in the midst of my worst times?
- Which young people in my community need this same lavish forgiveness and acceptance?

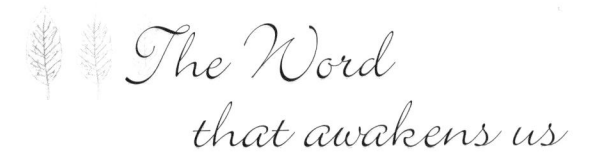
The Word
that awakens us

Scripture Passage

They said to each other, "Were not our hearts burning [within us] while he spoke to us on the way and opened the scriptures to us?"

(Luke 24:32)

Meditation

What young people are often looking for in adults is a sense of passion. At this point in their lives, they respond to people who are passionate about their vocation, interests, and beliefs. We believe, like in the sharing of communion, that Christ is present in the proclamation of the Word. But the way young people (and the rest of us) usually hear the Word leaves them wondering about the conviction of their faith. The stories of the Bible, in both the Old and New Testament, give testimony to a pilgrim people, people who are passionate about their faith. We need to proclaim, share, and live this Word, these stories of salvation and redemption with a similar sense of joy, intensity, and fidelity.

Prayer

God,

you walk among us,

and you stir within us feelings, emotions,

and desires that we know only from you.

Help us to not be selfish with the gift of your love

but rather empower us to passionately share, testify, and proclaim,

with every source of energy that we can muster,

You—risen, present, and alive!

You—here, with us, and forgiving!

You—real, passionate, and caring!

Help us to not be shy

but to be filled to the brim with your Word;

the saving story that you have planted deep within us.

Amen.

Questions for Reflection

℮ What are my sources of passion and energy?

℮ How can I tap into those resources when I feel exhausted and cynical?

Why are we frightened?

Scripture Passage

While they were still speaking about this, [Jesus] stood in their midst and said to them, "Peace be with you." But they were startled and terrified and thought that they were seeing a ghost. Then he said to them, "Why are you troubled? And why do questions arise in your hearts? Look at my hands and my feet, that it is I myself. Touch me and see, because a ghost does not have flesh and bones as you can see I have." And as he said this, he showed them his hands and his feet. While they were still incredulous for joy and were amazed, he asked them, "Have you anything here to eat?" They gave him a piece of baked fish; he took it and ate it in front of them.

(Luke 24:36–43)

Meditation

All of us, young and old, spend far too much time living in fear. Fear often consumes and paralyzes us. Fear is a demon that keeps us from reverencing the sacredness of the moment. When we live in fear, our past becomes a memory of only regret and shame, and our future becomes a fantasy of worry and anxiety. Far too many young people are drowning in fear and worry at this world they see before them, and at their prospects for happiness and security. When they look at us, yes, they need to see our humanity and vulnerability, but they also need to see our faith and conviction that fear will not conquer our lives. Jesus offers not a way out of fear but a way *through* our anxiety and worry. The message is not a life free from suffering and fear but rather a promise of peace in the midst of the journey and a place of grace at the other side.

Prayer

God,
you alone are strength.
You alone are peace.
You, only you, can lead us through
the fear,
the tension,
the anxiety,
and that which can cripple and dismantle
our sense of self,
our sense of serenity,
and our belief and faith in the gift of love.
You, only you,
come be with us,
be with the young,
and bring us all to faith
in the destiny that you have for us.
Amen.

Questions for Reflection

℃ What are my fears in life?
℃ What are some of the fears that lurk in the lives of young people?

God will do anything to take care of us

Scripture Passage

"I am the good shepherd. A good shepherd lays down his life for the sheep. A hired man, who is not the shepherd and whose sheep are not his own, sees a wolf coming and leaves the sheep and runs away, and the wolf catches and scatters them. This is because he works for pay and has no concern for the sheep. I am the good shepherd, and I know mine and mine know me, just as the Father knows me and I know the Father; and I will lay down my life for the sheep. I have other sheep that do not belong to this fold. These also I must lead, and they will hear my voice, and there will be one flock, one shepherd. This is why the Father loves me, because I lay down my life in order to take it up again. No one takes it from me, but I lay it down on my own. I have power to lay it down, and power to take it up again. This command I have received from my Father."

(John 10:11–18)

Meditation

It is easy to take care of those who follow without question; it is easy to serve and help empower those who already know how to take care of themselves. But those who are vulnerable, those who lose their way, those who choose the wrong path at times are the challenge for all of us. Jesus shows us the way. We do more than help pave a path for our young people to follow—we lay down our lives, we inconvenience ourselves, we speak out on their behalf, we get out of the way and let them shine, and we use any power we may have to help them get a glimpse of the reign of God. If we truly love and care for our young people, we will be willing to sacrifice our own security and power to help them realize their dreams and potential.

Prayer

God,
you constantly shepherd us.
You constantly go out of your way
to find us,
to help us find ourselves,
and you bring us back to you.
Help us now to not lose our way
but to rediscover your care and guidance
in our lives.
Be with us,
all of us:
the strong and confident,
the scared and worrisome,
and all of us who get up each day
to face all of life's adventures.
Be with us, always.
Amen.

Questions for Reflection

℃ What do I need to sacrifice in order to help others?
℃ How can I more honestly rely on God's strength in my life?

# We must wash their feet

Scripture Passage

Fully aware that the Father had put everything into his power and that he had come from God and was returning to God, [Jesus] rose from supper and took off his outer garments. He took a towel and tied it around his waist. Then he poured water into a basin and began to wash the disciples' feet and dry them with the towel around his waist. He came to Simon Peter, who said to him, "Master, are you going to wash my feet?" Jesus answered and said to him, "What I am doing, you do not understand now, but you will understand later." Peter said to him, "You will never wash my feet." Jesus answered, "Unless I wash you, you will have no inheritance with me." Simon Peter said to him, "Master, then not only my feet, but my hands and head as well." Jesus said to him, "Whoever has bathed has no need except to have his feet washed, for he is clean all over; so you are clean, but not all." For he knew who would betray him; for this reason, he said, "Not all of you are clean."

So when he had washed their feet [and] put his garments back on and reclined at table again, he said to them, "Do you realize what I have done for you? You call me 'teacher' and 'master,' and rightly so, for indeed I am. If I, therefore, the master and teacher, have washed your feet, you ought to wash one another's feet. I have given you a model to follow, so that as I have done for you, you should also do."

(John 13:3–15)

Meditation

This story appears only in John's Gospel, while the other three evangelists have the more revered Last Supper narrative, which most believers hold dear as the origin of the Eucharist. But John gives us no less a clear institution of the meal of the covenant—that we need to do more than eat and be nourished together in the usual sense. We are called and provoked to be people of mission, to bend down in service, to humble ourselves for the sake of God's vision for our lives.

In washing the feet of his disciples, Jesus gave us the ministerial command of our Baptism, an example for us to follow and build upon. Yes, we need to cook and dine, but after we are filled and satisfied, we need to bend low and wash. Then we will truly share in the mission of Jesus, and hopefully our young people will follow the lead.

Prayer

God,
help me, help all of us to serve.
Help us all to remember
that our young people need much more than talk,
much more than pious homilies about love and service.
They need to see us literally
bending low, humbling ourselves, and embracing our own weaknesses.
Give us the courage and grace
to wash away their poor self-esteem, their bad choices,
and their fears and failures,
into the basin of your love.
Help us to be servants,
help us to get over ourselves and do ministry.
Not our ministry, but yours—
to bring all to the Good News of your love.
Amen.

Questions for Reflection

℮ What are the qualities of true service?
℮ Am I willing to humble myself for the sake of others?

Discipleship:
laying down one's life

Scripture Passage

No one has greater love than this, to lay down one's life for one's friends.

(John 15:13)

Meditation

Sometimes the Scriptures are pretty direct. They say what they mean. To serve is to suffer. To be a minister is not about being nice. To be a disciple requires the entirety of our lives; it demands that we respond with all that we have; it challenges us to take the path of unpopularity, to embrace passion and suffering. It means aligning ourselves with the cross of Christ. In addition to our own understanding of this, we need to preach the sometimes unpopular message of suffering, pain, and death to a generation who might not be open to hearing it. It means proclaiming a message of truth to an age-group that is bombarded with messages and signs that persuade them to embrace an easy way of life, to avoid the cross. At times, we need to share some tough love with young people, to help them understand that pain and suffering are part and parcel of life, and for certain, at the center of what it means to follow Christ. This kind of love is hard for them, for all of us, to swallow. But it is this very kind of love that God calls us to share, sing, and celebrate.

Prayer

God,
we know and believe
that there can be no greater love
than to lay down our life for our friends.
You did so,
and you call us to do the same.
The road and task is hard,
but we believe that you have the strength for us to endure;
for all of us to be in service to all.
Help us to embrace this kind of love,
a love that knows no bounds,
a love that is not cheap
but is full of promise.
Love us well
so that we too can be this love to the world.
Amen.

Questions for Reflection

℮ Am I willing to embrace suffering and the cross?

℮ How am I teaching the message of suffering and sacrifice to young people?

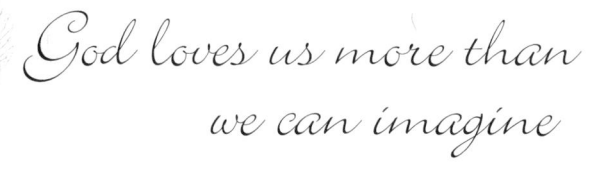

God loves us more than we can imagine

Scripture Passage

What then shall we say to this? If God is for us, who can be against us? He who did not spare his own Son but handed him over for all of us, how will he not also give us everything else along with him? Who will bring a charge against God's chosen ones? It is God who acquits us. Who will condemn? It is Christ [Jesus] who died, rather, was raised, who also is at the right hand of God, who indeed intercedes for us. What will separate us from the love of Christ? Will anguish, or distress, or persecution, or famine, or nakedness, or peril, or the sword? . . .

No, in all these things we conquer overwhelmingly through him who loved us. For I am convinced that neither death, nor life, nor angels, nor principalities, nor present things, nor future things, nor powers, nor height, nor depth, nor any other creature will be able to separate us from the love of God in Christ Jesus our Lord.

(Romans 8:31–35,37–39)

Meditation

It is difficult to imagine a God who loves us in this way. It seems naive, almost silly. Regardless of our age, our upbringing, our economic status, our standing in the community, we all have been let down; we all have experienced betrayal; we all have been victims of broken promises and dashed dreams; we all have been told we are loved, only to have that love turned into rejection and judgment. Unconditional love is something that we can never fully accomplish in our giving or receiving. But nonetheless, Jesus Christ destroys and re-creates what would seem impossible. Jesus never gives up on us, never abandons us, and never, never banishes us to hopelessness. Somehow, some way, our efforts need to help proclaim this wonderful truth to our young people. Perhaps the place we need to begin is with ourselves. If we cannot find even some glimpse of that "Christ love" in our own lives, if we cannot name or feel that presence when we fail, how can we possibly spread the message to young people? Christ is with us, always, and the love of Christ is anything but absent.

Prayer

God,
I really have a hard time believing that you love me,
regardless of how I act, regardless of how I have sinned,
regardless of how I have not loved others in return.
Yet you ask me to believe that you are still here, no matter what.
Melt my heart, break down my pride and cynicism,
and help me to receive this love,
a love that you so lavishly want to give me,
but a love that I find difficult to believe.
Help my unbelief so that I may feel your presence.
Then I can truly help the young people
whom you have entrusted to my care,
to find out that you are more than a mirage.
They need to know, feel, and experience that you are real.
Open our hearts and minds to see your love more clearly.
Amen.

Questions for Reflection

℮ Do I really believe that God loves me, no matter what?
℮ What are the things that block me from this love?

 *We are the Body of Christ*

Scripture Passage

For I received from the Lord what I also handed on to you, that the Lord Jesus on the night when he was betrayed took a loaf of bread, and when he had given thanks, he broke it and said, "This is my body that is for you. Do this in remembrance of me." In the same way he took the cup also, after supper, saying, "This is the new covenant in my blood. Do this, as often as you drink it, in remembrance of me." For as often as you eat this bread and drink the cup, you proclaim the Lord's death until he comes.

(1 Corinthians 11:23–26)

Meditation

We must remember that the most profound and lavish gift given to us by God was and is Jesus Christ. Jesus is one with God in his self-giving. Jesus gave us an everlasting meal and presence in his body and blood through the Eucharist. Each time we come forward to share the meal, may we always remember that this profound presence is more than just the elements that we receive; it is also the shared community. We share the meal not in isolation but in the context of a family who walks the journey with us. One of the greatest gifts our young people deserve to share in is the gift of one another, of the tribe of fellow sojourners who seek the same things in life: meaning, hope, love, and redemption. In the ritual act of the Eucharist, we enter into this most deep and wonderful mystery. We too are called to be broken and shared, poured out for one another, for in this sharing, we see, feel, experience, and become the Body of Christ.

Prayer

God,
help us,
and help our young people realize
and experience
your presence in the humble gifts
of bread and wine
and in the sharing of this sacred meal.
Be present in us.
Become real in us.
Transform and become for us
the body and blood of new life,
of the Kingdom,
and of life for the world.
Be here with us now.
Amen.

Questions for Reflection

℃ Do we as ministers sometimes minimize the Eucharist?

℃ How can we help name and celebrate the many ways that Christ is present in our lives?

# We all have gifts

Scripture Passage

There are different kinds of spiritual gifts but the same Spirit; there are different forms of service but the same Lord; there are different workings but the same God who produces all of them in everyone. To each individual the manifestation of the Spirit is given for some benefit.

(1 Corinthians 12:4–7)

Meditation

One of the saddest things that young people engage in is the constant comparing of themselves to their peers. They far too often see themselves not for who they are but for how they are in comparison or contrast to someone else who they believe is either better or worse. Our giftedness needs somehow to be seen on its own merits or, even more important, on the value that God places in us. God sees each of us as profoundly wonderful, and when we are able to truly choose to see that in everyone else, then God's creation can truly do its work. Young people desperately need to discover how absolutely wonderful they are in God's eyes and in our eyes as well. They struggle at times to hear God's voice affirming them, but if we speak out and affirm their giftedness, then the voice will be heard. We need to speak to, bless, encourage, and challenge them to realize that God has a plan for each and every one of them, and that their gifts are not to be hoarded for selfish purposes but are to be used to help create a vibrant and life-giving environment.

Prayer

God,

come now and send your Spirit,

fill us with your fire of love,

the passion that comes from you alone.

Activate in each and every one of us

the blessings and gifts that you have instilled

and planted in us.

Help us see our gift, help us release the gift, and help us share the gift.

What is the gift?

The gift is you, your presence.

The presence that we need, the presence that we ache for,

the presence that helps us to do more than just survive.

The presence that is true blessing, true resurrection, and true grace.

Be with us, now.

Amen.

Questions for Reflection

⌀ How can I embrace more fully the gifts of young people?

⌀ How can I help affirm young people in the midst of tremendous peer pressure?

What gifts are the most important?

Scripture Passage

Pursue love and strive for the spiritual gifts, and especially that you may prophesy. For those who speak in a tongue do not speak to other people but to God; for nobody understands them, since they are speaking mysteries in the Spirit. On the other hand, those who prophesy speak to other people for their upbuilding and encouragement and consolation. Those who speak in a tongue build up themselves, but those who prophesy build up the church.

(1 Corinthians 14:1–4)

Meditation

We so often misunderstand what being a prophet means. A prophet is not one who can foretell the future. In biblical understanding, a prophet is a spokesperson for God. Many of the gifts we develop we use for our own selfish purposes—for self-advancement or power. But the gift and challenge of prophecy is to speak out on God's behalf, and to build up God's people. Young people today have so many voices bombarding them—voices from the media, from the secular and sometimes shallow culture, from parental expectations, and from their own poor self-esteem and self-loathing. But do they hear God's voice? Who is transmitting that voice, that message to them in their complicated and conflicted lives? That is our call—to listen to the holy in our lives and to speak out on God's behalf. Our young people need to hear a better voice, and we cannot sit back and let someone else do the talking for their own self-grandiosity. We have to speak for the sake of young people, not for our own sake. This is true ministry.

Prayer

God,
you have blessed me, and you have blessed all of us
with gifts, with treasures, with opportunities beyond measure.
Help me to remember that these gifts are given with only
one mandate and condition from you:
To share them and to use them to speak and proclaim loudly
the wonder of your name and your presence and handiwork.
I still feel too young, and the young people around me
will always seem too young to be your prophets.
But you call us just the same.
Help me. Help all of us to say yes.
Then the Church, your Body of Christ on Earth,
can be born and flourish.
Amen.

Questions for Reflection

𝒞 What can I do to get over myself and my unworthiness in order to reach out and serve?

𝒞 How can I as an adult leader set better priorities for my family, community, parish, or school?

Keep Christ at the center

Scripture Passage

But may I never boast except in the cross of our Lord Jesus Christ, through which the world has been crucified to me, and I to the world.

(Galatians 6:14)

Meditation

Let us always remember that it is not about us, it is about Christ Jesus and his promise for us all. We often brag and boast about what we think is our ministry. This is a dangerous path and attitude. It is not our ministry. It is the ministry of Christ, the ministry of the Church. Let us take on the same attitude as Paul does in this Scripture passage. May we keep pointing beyond ourselves to Christ and his mission. When we do this, the blindness can be removed from our eyes and hearts, and we can serve more directly, more honestly, and, for sure, with greater love.

Prayer

God,
there is only you.
You are the center of my life,
you are the heartbeat of all that I am,
all that I give,
and all that I hope to be.
You are the beginning, the end,
and everything in between.
Come now, fill my heart,
be the fullness of my cup,
be the Word alive in my heart and mind,
and be the path for all my service.
Keep me focused,
filled with you, always.
Amen.

Questions for Reflection

𝒞 How do I define *ministry*?
𝒞 How can I develop a more concrete sense of mission in ministry
   with young people?

 *Intimacy with Christ*

Scripture Passage

So then you are no longer strangers and aliens, but you are citizens with the saints and also members of the household of God, built upon the foundation of the apostles and prophets, with Christ Jesus himself as the cornerstone. In him the whole structure is joined together and grows into a holy temple in the Lord; in whom you also are built together spiritually into a dwelling place for God.

(Ephesians 2:19–22)

Meditation

Wow! What other God would choose to associate with humanity? This God truly communes and stands by our side in a covenant of solidarity. Our God is truly intimate with us because God chose to take on our form and experience our hurts, fears, joys, ecstasies, victories, and failures. God is not far away watching us from a distance. The God of our faith is a God strongly connected to us, in love with us, in a deep, committed relationship on a daily basis, over the long haul. More than that, we share in God's glory. We are named saints. Often our young people feel that they have to earn this love, this status. This thinking is wrong. By the fact that God called them into being, God has named them "members of the household of God," "holy temples in the Lord." Our call is to help build the young people into community, to put them up on the pedestal of God's dwelling place. We can do this. We must do this.

Prayer

God,
by our own actions,
we cut ourselves off from you.
By our own selfishness and sinfulness,
we have alienated ourselves from you,
ourselves, and one another.
But by your actions,
by your presence,
you call us into a friendship,
a relationship so awesome,
so wonderful,
so undeserved
that we can hardly believe it to be true.
You are here, close by.
You are here, in all things.
You are here, calling us to be family with you.
Thank you, God.
Thank you for helping us all
to be a part of your home.
Amen.

Questions for Reflection

⌒ How do I keep God at a distance?
⌒ What are the things that alienate and isolate young people?

 *Time to grow up*

Scripture Passage

We may no longer be infants, tossed by waves and swept along by every wind of teaching arising from human trickery, from their cunning in the interests of deceitful scheming. Rather, living the truth in love, we should grow in every way into him who is the head, Christ, from whom the whole body, joined and held together by every supporting ligament, with the proper functioning of each part, brings about the body's growth and builds itself up in love.

(Ephesians 4:14–16)

Meditation

Our young people do not want to stay teenagers—they want to grow up. Deep down, they do not want us to be their age, for that is to be truly phony on our part. They want us to be our age. They want and need us to be older. They want to see how we live, how we make choices, and how we live with or without integrity. When they see us being honestly who we are, they have something to truly look up to. Not that they should be cloned in our image and likeness—not at all. They hopefully look up to us and want to emulate not the specifics of our lives but the greater model of how we live in faith and fidelity to our beliefs and to God's plan for us. That is what it means to be a mentor: to be ourselves, to grow up.

Prayer

God,
help me be me.
Help me and help all of us be authentic, true,
and faithful to the unique individuals we all are.
Help us see this uniqueness as the cornerstone of true community,
of real and honest maturity, of lives filled with integrity and purpose.
Help me relax and not try so hard to be a role model.
Just help me live and be myself.
Then young people and others will see what you see—
something special, something gifted—
and then hopefully they will see the possibilities for themselves.
Help me be me.
Amen.

Questions for Reflection

℘ Am I real and authentic with young people?

℘ What are the best qualities and skills that I need to develop more
   fully as a youth minister?

Never stop being thankful and creative

Scripture Passage

Rejoice always. Pray without ceasing. In all circumstances give thanks, for this is the will of God for you in Christ Jesus. Do not quench the Spirit.

(1 Thessalonians 5:16–19)

Meditation

An enduring quality that we constantly need to nurture in our lives and in ministry is the gift of gratitude. When we are grateful, we remain creative. When we are thankful, jealousy and pettiness melt away. When we are filled with gratitude, selfishness and narcissism leave our hearts. When we are in touch with the many blessings in our lives, we loathe hurting another. When we are a thankful people, we become our best selves. Young people experience too much negativity, gossip, sarcasm, and hopelessness in their lives these days. Let's give them an alternative. Let's show them another approach, a better way to live each day. First, let us hold close to our hearts the sense of honor and privilege we feel in being in their midst. Then let us make sure they can see that from us in our actions and words. When they receive this kind of precious gift from us, their spirit will not be quenched at all. It will flow like a living stream of joy.

Prayer

God,

help us all let go of our ego, our anger, our pettiness,

our whining, our jealousies, all of our negativity.

Help us move beyond seeing what we do not have,

toward seeing how wonderful you are, how lavishly you love us,

and how fortunate and blessed we really are.

Let the young see in our lives

true joy and gratitude for your presence.

Come and penetrate the darkness of our cynicism.

Awaken in us the call to delight in our lives,

in one another, just as you do when you see us.

Help us remember that there is truly a reason to rejoice.

That reason is you.

Amen.

Questions for Reflection

⌾ What am I thankful for in my life?

⌾ What are the things that get in the way of my being a person of gratitude?

# We need to set an example

Scripture Passage

For you know how one must imitate us. For we did not act in a disorderly way among you, nor did we eat food received free from anyone. On the contrary, in toil and drudgery, night and day we worked, so as not to burden any of you. Not that we do not have the right. Rather, we wanted to present ourselves as a model for you, that you might imitate us.

(2 Thessalonians 3:7–9)

Meditation

We need to live our lives fully, with integrity and intention, but we must not be afraid to make mistakes and even fail at times. To live—that is our call. We will have an influence with young people if we live our lives passionately, if we take a stand on issues, if we live beyond minimal breathing, walking, and talking. God gave us life. In other words, being pro-life is more than being against abortion. Being pro-life means to live with energy and intention. When we do that, those in our care will have something to live for. God wants that for them, for all of us. So should we.

Prayer

God,
give me the wisdom and the desire
to live—fully and completely.
Help me to show the young people in my care
that life need not be boring or meaningless.
Help us all to remember
that you have given us so much to live for,
and so much to celebrate.
Help me be passionate in my life,
to take a stand,
to help those I lead
seize and discover joy in their lives,
rather than live in suspicion and shadow.
Plant within me that desire to live in truth
so that all may see you in all things.
Amen.

Questions for Reflection

⟳ How do I learn and grow from my mistakes?

⟳ What am I passionate about when it comes to young people?

 *Faith*

Scripture Passage

I am grateful to God, whom I worship with a clear conscience as my ancestors did, as I remember you constantly in my prayers, night and day. I yearn to see you again, recalling your tears, so that I may be filled with joy, as I recall your sincere faith that first lived in your grandmother Lois and in your mother Eunice and that I am confident lives also in you. For this reason, I remind you to stir into flame the gift of God that you have.

(2 Timothy 1:3–6)

Meditation

Faith is not faith if it is kept to oneself; it must be shared. For most of us, our faith has been nurtured and sustained not by our catechisms, our professions of faith, or the keeping of religious practices but rather by its being passed on to us from those who have journeyed before us. Not from books, but rather from parents, teachers, mentors, and heroes who saw the spark and potential within us—this is where the treasure of our belief and sustained faith finds its origins. In many cases young people today do not have as many built-in human resources to share the story. So, our task and our charge are even greater when we try to evangelize, catechize, and celebrate our faith with young people. We need to recall the stories of faith that have sustained us, and pass them on.

Prayer

God,
I praise and thank you with all my heart
for the wonderful people you have placed in my life:
parents, teachers, and so many others
who provided light and promise for me.
You call me to be that same light and promise
for the young and fragile, who are in need of wisdom.
I know that I am not worthy, but I also know that you are calling me
to be your voice, to share the story, and to help bring forth your light.
Give me the strength, increase my faith,
and push me beyond myself so that I may faithfully be your servant
to the young of age and of heart.
Be with me on this journey, now and always.
Amen.

Questions for Reflection

- As I look back through my life, who were the people who inspired me by their faith?
- My life is a story of faith. How am I passing that on to young people?

Our young people are chosen by God

Scripture Passage

But you are "a chosen race, a royal priesthood, a holy nation, a people of his own, so that you may announce the praises" of him who called you out of darkness into his wonderful light.

> Once you were "no people"
>> but now you are God's people.

(1 Peter 2:9–10)

Meditation

Many of us, including young people, have a difficult time seeing ourselves as ministers. When we think of ministers, we usually think of the ordained, or those who have made specific, more institutional kinds of promises or vows. And yet, our Baptism is exactly this: a call to ministry. Worthiness is not the issue—it never is with God. God does not work that way; rather, God calls the flawed, the imperfect, the sinner to this royal priesthood, to greater communion with God and God's people. We are chosen whether we like it or not. While we at times feel compelled to run the other way, God keeps turning us back to the light—the light of new life, new possibilities. Young people are looking for direction, searching to find their destiny, their calling. Maybe we can help them, not through coercion but through amplifying and affirming in them the light and holiness we see in them.

Prayer

God,
you persist, you are relentless, and you keep calling me.
Help me to weaken, and let your Word and your voice
overtake me and live in me.
Open the doors of my heart
so that I may accept your blessing in my life
and respond by serving you.
May I always see the grace and gifts
that you have placed in the young.
Help me see past their lack of years and wisdom
so that I may experience their passion and outrageous energy,
so that I may be transformed by their heart and soul,
so that in their youthful approach,
I may come to know you in a fresh way.
Amen.

Questions for Reflection

C How do I see myself as one of God's chosen people?
C What are the ways that I can learn to let go, listen, and hear God's voice?

Love is the center

Scripture Passage

Above all, let your love for one another be intense, because love covers a multitude of sins. Be hospitable to one another without complaining. As each one has received a gift, use it to serve one another as good stewards of God's varied grace. Whoever preaches, let it be with the words of God.

(1 Peter 4:8–11)

Meditation

While at times it sounds redundant and cliché, love truly is the center of our call. Love is a very simple and clear command, and yet our ability to practice it and live it is difficult and elusive for many of us. Why is that? Perhaps it is because the call to love cannot tolerate jealousy; it cannot stomach gossip, competition, or greed. And for some reason, those demons so often win because they can give us, in the short term, a sense of security and power. But this sense of security and power wanes very quickly. In ministering with youth, we must be careful. Young people are susceptible to our choices, words, and behavior. Our age difference and position give us a power and influence over young people, whether we accept it or not. When our young people succeed, we must shower them with love. When they fail (and they will), our response must be the same: love. Always love, regardless of their successes or failures, regardless of whether they live up to our expectations, regardless of the path they choose. Love—it is the only way.

Prayer

God,
you love us so much,
for you have given us the greatest gift:
Jesus—yourself, your very essence,
your very Son.
Help us to give to young people
the very same gift of your love—
the love of sacrifice,
the love that conquers sin and death,
the love that gives meaning
to our very existence.
Shower us with this love
so that we can give what we have received
and be more like you.
Amen.

Questions for Reflection

- When I speak, whose voice do young people hear?
- Which young people in my community most need my unconditional love, even when they disappoint others?

Our young people truly know God

Scripture Passage

I write to you, children,
  because you know the Father.
I write to you, fathers,
  because you know him who is from the beginning.
I write to you, young people,
  because you are strong
  and the word of God abides in you,
    and you have overcome the evil one.

(1 John 2:14)

Meditation

Our youth have so much to give, so much to offer, and yes, so much wisdom to share with us, an aging, sometimes cynical Church. They can be strong and youthful in their bodies, and they can be strong and inspiring in their faith as well. We can see it and experience it if we open our eyes, ears, and hearts to what is before us. God is there. God is present in young people's succeeding and also in their blundering, staggering, and stammering. Young people are wonderful, living, youthful manifestations of "God-with-us," and they are often waiting for us to listen and be open to receive what they have to offer. We have much to share with them as well. Let us not hold out on them, but let us, without hesitation, share and bestow what we know—that God is alive, real, and here for all of us.

Prayer

God,
help me to get over myself
and to come to realize and own the insight
that you have planted within me.
You know me well,
and you are eager for me to know you too.
Help open up the network between you and me.
Empower me to remember
that you are near
and that your love for me is strong.
Keep me safe, and draw me close to you.
Amen.

Questions for Reflection

- How can I open myself more to see the goodness in young people?
- How can we as a Church share the wonderful reality of God more passionately?

Make all things new

Scripture Passage

"Behold, I make all things new."

(Revelation 21:5)

Meditation

With every generation comes the promise of new life, new and fresh ideas and insight, and fresh possibilities for growth and renewal. That same possibility for growth is present and alive in every young person we come in contact with. Young people are eager. They are champing at the bit to influence, lead, and stake their claim in their journey of life. We need not be afraid of this, as we often can be. Rather we should rejoice and trust the Spirit to do its work with these wonderful, young, and gifted saints of God. Every generation of young people has a vision, some more dramatic than others, some more well thought out than others, but nonetheless, they have a vision. God will lead the young people. God took care and loved them long before they were ever in our care. We also need to have faith that God will continue to watch out for them after they leave our surroundings. So, what will we do with the time that we have with them? Hopefully we give them permission to shine with their possibilities for greatness, not greatness for power and achievement but rather greatness of purpose, greatness of love, and greatness in their need for and dependence on God.

Prayer

God,
you are always making all things new.
Mold us, shape us,
and let your spirit breathe deep in us.
Open our humanity to receive the mystery
and blessedness of your love, of your plan,
of your vision for our lives.
Be our present and future,
be our today and tomorrow,
and be the keeper of our dreams.
Come now.
Make all things new.
Amen.

Questions for Reflection

- What can I do to integrate prayer more intimately into my faith life and ministry?
- How can we as a community, parish, or school be more open to the energy and new life that young people have to offer?

Scriptural index

Acknowledgments *(continued from copyright page)*

The Scripture passage on page 16 is from *Prayers Before an Awesome God,* by David Haas (Winona, MN: Saint Mary's Press, 1998), page 73.

The Scripture passages on pages 18, 21, 24, 28, 36, 64, 66, 70, and 84 are from the New Revised Standard Version of the Bible, Catholic Edition. Copyright © 1993 and 1989 by the Division of Christian Education of the National Council of the Churches of Christ in the United States of America. All rights reserved.

The Scripture passages on pages 26 and 34 are from the New Jerusalem Bible. Copyright © 1985 by Darton, Longman and Todd, London, and Doubleday, a division of Bantam Doubleday Dell Publishing Group, New York. All rights reserved.

All other Scripture passages contained herein are from the New American Bible with Revised New Testament and Revised Psalms. Copyright © 1991, 1986, and 1970 by the Confraternity of Christian Doctrine, Washington, DC. Used by the permission of the copyright owner. All rights reserved. No part of the New American Bible may be reproduced in any form without permission in writing from the copyright owner.